# The Ley Lines of the Soul

Other books by this author:

*Marrow of Flame, Poems of the Spiritual Journey* (Hohm Press)

*A Cloth of Fine Gold, Poems of the Inner Journey* (Lulu Press)

*Unmasking the Rose, A Record of a Kundalini Initiation* (Hampton Roads Publishing Company)

(All of above are available on Amazon)

# The Ley Lines of the Soul

Poems of Ecstasy and Ascension

DOROTHY WALTERS

Copyright © 2012 by Dorothy Walters.
Photography and cover design by N. M. Rai

ISBN:     Softcover     978-1-4691-5318-6

All rights reserved. No part of this book may be reproduced or transmitted in any form or by any means, electronic or mechanical, including photocopying, recording, or by any information storage and retrieval system, without permission in writing from the copyright owner.

This is a work of fiction. Names, characters, places and incidents either are the product of the author's imagination or are used fictitiously, and any resemblance to any actual persons, living or dead, events, or locales is entirely coincidental.

This book was printed in the United States of America.

**To order additional copies of this book, contact:**
Xlibris Corporation
1-888-795-4274
www.Xlibris.com
Orders@Xlibris.com

# CONTENTS

Preface..................................................................................................xi
Ley Lines ............................................................................................xiii
What Is Sacred Poetry?......................................................................xiii

## PART ONE
*The Longing For Angels*

Before....................................................................................................3
Who You Are.........................................................................................4
More.......................................................................................................5
Looking..................................................................................................6
How to See an Angel............................................................................7
The Visitant..........................................................................................9
Whatever You Offer...........................................................................10
The Seeker Attempts to Return.......................................................11
Full Face..............................................................................................12
Whatever You Do...............................................................................13
Awakenings........................................................................................14
The Mystery.......................................................................................15
What I Now Perceived......................................................................16
Some Kiss...........................................................................................17

## PART TWO
*The Embrace*

Betrothed............................................................................................21
What I Can Tell You..........................................................................23
Bliss.....................................................................................................24
Nobody Understands This...............................................................25

Almost Dawn ............................................................................26
The Surprise ...........................................................................27
Love Poems for the Invisible ................................................28
This Love ................................................................................31
Great Lovers...........................................................................32
The Flower .............................................................................34
The Beckoning ......................................................................35
What? .....................................................................................36
The Heart In Mourning ........................................................37
Beatrice In Rapture ...............................................................38
Last Year ................................................................................39
Still More Love Poems to the Invisible Within ..................40
Apology ..................................................................................45
Christian Mystics ..................................................................46
Particles Dancing ..................................................................47
The Cellular Level ................................................................48
Hymn to the Nameless One ................................................50
The Ley Lines of the Soul....................................................51

## PART THREE
*How To See An Angel*

Even if you have Trudged ...................................................55
In a Strange Tongue .............................................................56
After ........................................................................................57
St. Teresa Reflects On Her Raptures...................................58
Two Riddles ..........................................................................59
The Dissident ........................................................................60
After All .................................................................................61
Buddhists................................................................................63
Enough ...................................................................................65
Stones Piled One Above the Other on the Shore .............66
Sea Change............................................................................67
Spanda Karika .......................................................................68
Everything Moving ...............................................................69
Ever Arriving ........................................................................70
About Nothing ......................................................................71
If you are a Mystic ...............................................................73

Before we Came..........................................................................74
As Silk to Coarse Fiber ...............................................................75
What the Angel Said ...................................................................76
If you Want.................................................................................78
The Lives of the Soul..................................................................79
The Awakening ..........................................................................80
Karma..........................................................................................82
What to Think of Before Dying ..................................................83
Dancing with the Great Lion......................................................85
The Angel....................................................................................86
Going Beyond .............................................................................87

Author's Note..............................................................................89

This book is dedicated to Kathy Fowler,
Karen Lester, N. M. Rai, Maggie Powell, and
Stephanie Marohn, all of whom offered inspiration
and support and held candles aloft as I moved
forward along the "ley lines" of this project.

It is also dedicated especially to all who
work alone with the Beloved Within,
the invisible partner in the long dance.

# Preface

When I was 53 years old and living in Kansas as a university professor of English and Women's Studies, I had an experience that changed my life forever. In fact, in the words of Katherine Anne Porter, it was "the moment that changed everything." Because I have described this experience elsewhere in some detail (see "Unmasking the Rose: a Record of a Kundalini Initiation" and other sources), I will not go into the actual circumstances and consequences here; suffice it to say that what I underwent was a sudden, massive, and swift arousal of the Kundalini energies, which shot from my base to my crown, which opened in ecstatic bliss as "a thousand petals unfolding." At that moment I knew, beyond all doubt, that each of us is indeed simply a tiny particle in this vast energy source that engenders and in fact comprises all that exists.

This was a profound revelation for someone who had never practiced Eastern techniques, such as meditation or yoga or even Tai Chi. In fact, at that time (1981), such approaches were virtually unknown in my part of the world, as was Kundalini itself. I was instantly transported into supreme bliss, underwent visionary (inner) initiation into what I later discovered were the traditions of Tibetan Buddhism and Kashmiri Shaivism, and found myself totally transformed from who I thought I was into the initial formulation of who I was to become.

The bliss did not go away, but continued to visit regularly for many years thereafter (accompanied by intermittent periods of pain as the body adjusted to these new frequencies.)

I had no teacher or guru to lead me, so I was mostly left to my own devices. Each morning I performed a simple ceremony of devotion, and each time it was as though the room (and I) were filled with divine, flowing, celestial ecstasy, as if we were lifted into another realm where rapture was the norm. I came to think of these sweet intervals of heightened awareness as times of "bliss consciousness," and wrote many poems and prose reflections on these recurrent episodes of union with the Beloved Within. I was stunned to realize that the latter term is indeed not a metaphor, but rather an apt description for those interludes when one feels truly and completely united with the unseen paramour, God as lover.

The poetry of the Middle and Far East frequently refers to God not as Father, or Mother, or even Friend, but rather as the Beloved, This perspective now made total sense to me (see Rumi, Kabir, Hafiz, or Mirabai for examples). Now I too found how it was to be coupled with an invisible mate (think of the nuns who become "brides of Christ," the many milkmaids who are wooed by the god Krishna in the lore of ancient India) and how, in a very literal sense, one's very identity is fused with that unseen, yet extremely palpable presence.

Several of the poems which follow use traditional quasie-rotic imagery to depict such love of human and divine. These allusions, though often extremely sensuous, are not to be confused with sensual descriptions of ordinary love making. They go well beyond that mundane level, for they are in fact spiritual phenomena not only in origin but in outcome. They represent the sublimation of "ordinary" love into its highest form, the bliss of transcendent union with the unseen Beloved in a manner that all of us will (I believe) know, either here or at the moment of transition, for, according to many near death accounts, the Beloved within is there ready to receive and transform us in absolute love when we cross into the other realm.

Many believe that these "bliss energies" are the mechanism by which humanity itself will be reshaped and thus ascend to a higher plane on the ladder of evolution. I happen to concur with this outlook, for, having gone though the fire and emerged intact, I now believe that anything can happen to anyone at any time, and that, in fact, the great transmutation of earth and its inhabitants is already well underway.

Boulder, Colorado
January, 2012

*(For those interested in a fuller description of my Kundalini initiation, see my blog at www.kundalinisplendor.blogspot. com as well as "Unmasking the Rose, A Record of a Kundalini Initiation.")*

# LEY LINES
## (Definition)

Ley lines are invisible energy lines that run below
the surface of the earth and mark various sacred sites
and settlements along their trajectory.

I think of them as the unseen threads that connect
each of us to others as well as to divine source.

# WHAT IS SACRED POETRY?

Sacred Poetry is the ongoing effort of the soul to capture
in syllables the relation of the self to the larger reality
which we call the divine. It seeks to outline in graspable
ways the connection of the mortal to the immortal,
the confined to the boundless. It is the arriving spirit's
lament for the lost paradise, and its celebration of
recurrent joy at its earthly home.

Poetry issues from the realm of the mysterious,
that region which resides within us all but which we
can explore only through indirect and imprecise means.
This realm is not available for direct scrutiny.
Occasionally we catch strains of its distant song,
or stumble upon fragments of its secret messages.
When this happens, we call it a poem.

Poetry weaves the ley lines of the soul.

# PART ONE

# THE LONGING FOR ANGELS

# BEFORE

*"Before I was named I belonged to you."*
*Rilke*

Wherever I was, hidden in your thigh,
a sycamore seed waiting
in earth,
a thought preparing to leap forth,
I had no name.
My body had no shape.
My eyes were not yet
opened.
Even my face was dark.
What are the features
of that which does not exist?
Nonetheless, I was yours,
an unmarked impulse,
a treasure you carried
like a charm
hung from your vest,
before you sent me
down.

# WHO YOU ARE

How the body is put together,
with its tender fastenings,
its mysterious openings,
its muscles working in
smooth coordination
to convey it
where it wishes to go,
how it changes
from year to year,
from day to day,
its cells working in collusion
to carry it always
into a new configuration,
how the face communicates
its signals
wherever it goes,
whether it is
happy or sad
or puzzled
or plotting,
how the inner and outer,
organs and coverings are part
of the same being,
the same oneness
that is bound together
to make the unique creation,
the one combination
that is you,
present here, now,
spirit's abode,
soul's habitation,
never to be encountered
again in time's endless cycles.

## MORE

No matter what they tell
us,
we know there is always
more.
The Big Bang made a great noise,
(had anyone been there
to hear it),
and after that,
icy fragments,
spewing fires,
amoebae, fins,
dinosaurs,
green things growing from earth,
climbing creatures with tails and feet,
everything leading to
where we are now,
how we got here,
impossibility born
of a million improbabilities,
the vastly large
coupled
with the infinitely small,
twinkle in daddy's eye,
one out of a billion
swimmers
making it home.

## LOOKING

We go on our wanderings,
looking here,
seeking there,
turning over this leaf
or stone,
scrutinizing the clouds
for a message,
sometimes just stopping
and listening carefully.

Don't you ever get tired
of this endless searching,
this fruitless pursuit of a sign?
Don't you sometimes long
for a final revelation,
angels descending on
a cloud,
the ultimate "aha!"

What would you do
if you made a sudden discovery,
the light surrounding you
like a revelation,
heavenly choirs
singing hosanna?

Would you be happier then?
Could you cope
with this amazed wildness
touching your cells alive,
reminding you
that you, too, are stardust,
pulsation in the eternal flow?

# HOW TO SEE AN ANGEL

Stand very still.
Don't breathe,
or if you do,
do it silently.

Be in a familiar place,
or else a new place
which feels familiar.

Under a tree by
running water.
Or else in a church
or temple,
where vibrations of
the holy still linger
in the air.

Incense and candles are
fine,
but not required.

If you know a prayer
or a mantra,
this is the time.

Music will help.
Especially kirtans
or hymns.

Look around
for bits of color,
small flashes of light.

Close your eyes
for one brief moment,
then open and turn very slowly.

Listen for something that
sounds like a wooden flute
playing in the distance.

You will feel a
quiet breeze pass over you.
Your cells will brighten,
and you will give a little sigh.

That is when it will happen.
There will be a soft rush of wings.
a blur of shining movement . . .
Everything will light up
as if you are standing
in a cloud of sweet feeling.

Now look straight ahead:
an image will appear
at the corner of your eye,
white wings hovering against
a field of blue and gold . . .

Your heart will open
and you will become
as if two lovers kissing

When you awaken,
you will find
a single feather
in your hand.

# THE VISITANT

For what is an angel,
after all?
Is it oneself,
cast into its
larger dimensions,
swelling with joy
and attentiveness?

Or is it truly
presence from
some other nameless realm,
region of
that place where
Mystery dwells?

And if it should come before us,
massive, bright,
how might we greet it,
bear its gaze,
its knowingness
of who we are,
each particle of secret longing,
each hidden scar?

## WHATEVER YOU OFFER

Whatever you offer me,
I will take it.

I don't need bribes
to swallow
the bread and honey of your love.

This wine needs no water
to wash it down.

Even if we must perform
the many labors,
or huddle in
the darkened corners
of the caves
for eons
as the silence thickens
and the glaciers
gather.

This is what we have
hungered for
for so many days
for so many years.

# THE SEEKER ATTEMPTS TO RETURN

I could, of course, put
a mark
on my forehead
(and don't think
I wouldn't like
to do this)

or I might wander
about in a robe
of saffron or maroon
(and never believe
I wouldn't wish
to clothe myself this way.)

I could stand beneath
a tree
and recite ancient verses,
give blessings as
someone with strange eyes
fondles a flute
or a stringed instrument
nearby
(and I would do this gratefully,
indeed I would.)

I could infuse the crowd
with sweetness,
love energy from God
and watch them cry out,
and fall to the ground.
Now I have only silence

sometimes these words,
dream passages
from that other world
that I say to myself
at night.
Shanti, shanti, shanti

## FULL FACE

*"Every happiness is the child of a separation*
*it did not think it could survive."*
*Rilke*

Accept it,
even when it turns to you
full face.

Do not turn away,
when it invites you
to enter into unknown embraces,
shadow realms,
breathes its breath
like a coy animal
on your unsuspecting nape.

What is entering
is what has always been,
a reality beyond
your own small
imagining,
something greater,
more profound
than your
familiar, bounded dwelling place.

## WHATEVER YOU DO

Whatever you do,
don't waste your time
struggling with issues
about "faith" and
whether "the Other" is real
or not.

Do not worry about
your own existence—
whether you are palpable
or just a mirage
floating in a mirror.

When the worthies
begin debating such things inside
the temple,
do not bow and listen.
Run outside,
rattle the windows,
storm the doors,
let the music of light
come in.

Better still,
turn them out
into the sun,
point their solemn faces
toward the trees
blooming in fall's
swelling luminosity,
let them see how
brilliant

is a leaf
falling gracefully
into its new incarnation,
how majestic the limbs
in their bright emerging configurations.

## AWAKENINGS

Some do it quickly,
like making love over
a short noon break,
lightning flash of illumination,
bursting nova
in the brain.

Others take their time,
are sensuous,
meditative,
thoughtfully absorbing for years
the soft rays of love,
relishing each one.

Others try to follow a book
with its stages
and diagrams,
but they get lost
somewhere
between the
many charts
and prescriptions.
Who wants to
try to remember
how to breathe in a certain way
or count the petals of a lotus flower
when
making love?

Best to let it happen
in its own manner,
a sly spirit

winking down
from the ceiling,
a serious lover
come to call
when least expected.

# THE MYSTERY

Some come at it
with weights and measures,
some waving a sieve.

Some sing to it,
ballads and carols,
hoping to coax forth
its hidden center,
unwind the sheath
of who it is.

Some tap on it,
or deal heavy blows
with hammers,
trying to smash
its thick shield
force it to bow down.

Some seek ways to clamber in,
explore its hidden vaults
and chambers.

Some lie down beside it,
breathe its cool scent,
become its own self.

# WHAT I NOW PERCEIVED

*"Until I perceived it, no thing was complete."*
*Rilke*

So, what was it
I was looking for then.
Like entering a room
to find an object,
then forgetting
what it was
I came to find,
only odor of roses
clinging.

When I encountered the ultimate,
I thought searching
was over.
Everything complete
at last,
nothing more required.

Then I met one
who took apart
my theories,
my notions of who I was
crumbled around me
like walls of ancient cities
assaulted by time,
again I became
a captive of longing,
of seeking
what I now perceived.

## SOME KISS

*"There is some kiss we want with
our whole lives, the touch of
spirit on the body."*
*Rumi (Coleman Barks)*

Yes, of course,
that is the thing we want,
touch of spirit
on body,
delight of soul
enfleshed and opened,

trembling at last,
how could we not
remember
how it was before,
when you were not there,
when all we had
was this cloud of longing
and did not even know
what it was
we were looking for?

# PART TWO

# THE EMBRACE

## BETROTHED

*"So at the end of the day, we give thanks*
*for being betrothed to the unknown"*
*John O'Donohue*

However one looks at it,
it was not easy—
that bridal night,
mingling of self
and the unknown who appeared.

Everything took place
in secrecy and silence,
at the hidden center,
the core where presence
begins.

How do you mate
with something unseen?
Become one
with what has no form or name?

The days were filled with sweetness
and tumult,
nights so intense
that passion itself
became too pale a word.

The world unfolded
in endless celebration,
a constant feast to which
the heart said yes,
the spirit yearned.

Now, old lovers,
we live quietly,
sometimes meet
and nod in recognition,
remembrance of that special time,
when we no longer knew
who was lover, who beloved.

## WHAT I CAN TELL YOU

(for the Beloved Within)

What I can tell you
is only about
the bliss

The gurus and the priests,
they have their notions
and their theories.

It may all of it be true,
every single particle and proclamation.

But I know nothing
about such notions as these.

I know only the blinding moment
when the Lover arrives,
the sadness of
goodbye.

No one told me
how
to do this,
or how to share it
abroad with others.

Mine is a solitary
joy,
a single path
to the gateless
gate.

## BLISS

Sometimes it hurts a bit.
Like a new bride
getting deflowered
over and over.
But do not fret.

You will soon get used
to all this joy.

Your cells will take notice,
tell each other
what to do.

Now you are like a vase
overflowing with blossoms
and too much water.

# NOBODY UNDERSTANDS THIS

Nobody understands this
unless they have been there.
Traveled this rock strewn road,
fallen into this deep well.

How could you know how it is
to have your heart
eaten by a lion
unless you had heard
the lion's roar,
felt his clasp
upon your throat?

What could you imagine
about lost angels
floating down
on pulsing streams of light
unless your bed
was covered
in feathers
when you awoke?

## ALMOST DAWN

Almost dawn.
Once again,
you slipped in
while I was sleeping,
now you are demanding more.

What else can I give you?
My heart was the first to go.
When I heard your voice
I fainted and fell down dumb.
Each time you trembled through me,
you with no body,
no name,
a flame lit where I stood,
until I became a shadow,
a wraith consumed in fire.

Do you want these ashes?
Come,
hold out your hand.
We are mingled here
together
always.

## THE SURPRISE

She says, I am not ready for this.
It says, you have always been
    ready for this.

She says, I don't know where
    this is coming from.
It says, you know exactly where
    this is coming from.

She says, I don't know how
    to do this.
It says, you have always known
    how to do this.

She says, what will happen
    when you leave?
It says, I will never leave.
I am your body, brain,
    and blood,
I am the One of all.
I am your true core.

# LOVE POEMS FOR THE INVISIBLE

### They Speak

They speak of enlightenment.

Can darkness
dispel Darkness?
light illumine Light?

O, My Invisible,
you and I know the secret ways.

. . . . . . . . . . . . . . . . . . . . . . . . . . . . . . . . . . . .

### Out of Nowhere

When you first came
I was not prepared.
Lightning flash of love
arriving out of nowhere.

Now you enter more stealthily.
Sometimes you have stayed
the night
and I did not even know.

I still am not used
to your presence.
Lodger who
leaves no sign,
pays no rent.

## For So Many Years

How could I have known
this marriage would endure so long.
That you would remain faithful
for so many years.

I think this union
was meant to last.
Year after year,
your secret kisses,
my amazed silence.

. . . . . . . . . . . . . . . . . . . . . . . . . . . . . . . . . . . . . . . .

## Advaita

Yet why am I surprised
to find you still here
day after day,
year after year.
Lying beside me,
waiting for me to wake.
Stirring in my veins
even before I arise.
Walking where I walk.

You and I both know the
secret:
We are the same.
Two faces,

one body,
two players,
one stage.

This pledge
was made in other realms,
eons ago.
We set the terms
ourselves,

. . . . . . . . . . . . . . . . . . . . . . . . . . . . . . . . . . . . . . . . .

**Like a Mongolian**

Now you are arriving
just anywhere.

Like a Mongolian herdsman
who tackles his bride
on the steppe
and plants his flag to say,
"Here we are!"

Your horse, my mare,
what a combination.

## **THIS LOVE**

can consume you,
devour you,
drag you to the depths
where pearls float in the eyes
of the lost fishers,
blast you into
the outer regions
where there is no sound
but the frantic beating
of your own heart,
break you like brittle clay,
bend you like
molten iron,
wrap you around
your own belly,
turn your face
toward what
is ever shining,
waiting
for you to see.

*(The fourth line echoes the famous image of
Eliot's "Wasteland":
"Those are pearls/that were his eyes.")*

# GREAT LOVERS

Great lovers
do not hold back.
They give themselves
freely
the way an apple orchard
releases its fragrance
to anyone passing near
its scented blooms,
or a sunset
spreads its
scarlet radiance
over the water
for all to see.

But great lovers
do not accumulate
by numbers.
They do not measure their joy
by how many conquests,
count up the tally.

They return rather
to the same chamber,
the familiar patterns.
A subtle touching of hands
or lips
is often enough.
They understand Dante
and how it was
he dedicated his life
to a woman he never knew.
Or Rumi with Shams,

talking about the
Mystery of all things,
alone together.

Because great lovers
give themselves away,
they are often
shattered when their
only beloved disappears,
leaving them to
face their grief
alone on the moonless nights
when they search the heavens
in vain for a sign of comfort.
They are like gamblers
who risk all
at the tables,
winners for a while,
then losing everything
in one sudden turn.

There is but one
Beloved
who never leaves,
never turns away.
Only when you embrace
the Beloved Within
will you find constant love.

## THE FLOWER

This is an azalea.
It has no purpose other than
to make itself beautiful,
and so attract its
many lovers,
who come to gather from it
honey to carry on the winds
to other flowers, again
and again,
an endless sequence.

It is the many petaled god,
waiting for all of us
to gather close.

It wants to make love with us,
every single being,
every hour of day and night,
a gift to share.
That way we make each other
radiant and glowing.
Then we fly forth
and know
that we love and are loved.

## THE BECKONING

You called me
and I came down,
small soul wrapped
in the folds of the dark flower.

I arrived not knowing
where I had been,
whose voice had summoned,
why I had come.

How could I foresee
that this unfolding
would arrive
in such bliss,
body awakening again
to its own beginnings?

How could I guess
it would carry such pain,
always the throb of grief
pulsing through
the vein of joy?

## WHAT?

For a long while
bliss
lay hidden
inside me,
bright flame within a dark rock.

Now it is pain.
Light playing over water.

Are these two sides
of the same coin,
different ends of the same rainbow?

Two mysteries
wrapped around
each other
in a single packet,
waiting to be
opened.

## THE HEART IN MOURNING

Bring your gift to the door.
Even if all you have
is your sorrow,
the pain of the
flower crushed
in the road,
the child shivering
along the wayside.

Know that grief is enough.
Your offering
will be taken,
exalted
into the highest place.
The heart in mourning is
its own benediction.

## BEATRICE IN RAPTURE

Always she was alone.
Always there was silence,
the inner radiance.
What was it she was waiting for?

At times it came,
spreading across her shadow
like sunlight over an autumn floor,
entering where
there was no real way.
Sometimes there was only a
suspension of nothingness,
emptiness palpable as dust.

But still she waited.
Patience was the key.
Lost in a wilderness of hope,
the uncounted stations
of desire.

*(The Beatrice mentioned here was the beloved of Dante, who, although he never met her, turned her into the image of the ideal beloved and made her his guide into the heavenly regions in "The Divine Comedy.")*

## LAST YEAR

You may think I have done with you,
but, no, you are still with me—
like a Christmas treat that I savored
and still taste slightly on my tongue,
a jewel or a precious book
that someone left for me
under the tree,
a strain of music
that still plays in
my head.

True, we played our game
of ups and downs,
our dance of
wins and seeming losses,
everything balancing out
pretty much
at the end.

What you gave me
is yet to be catalogued
fully,
but I've got the gist of it
here,
like a package I carry around
under my arm,
its contents yet
to be assessed,
unknown at this point
to anyone
until I say "open sesame"
and release the string.

# STILL MORE LOVE POEMS TO THE INVISIBLE WITHIN

### 1.

**What I Have Given You**

What I have given you
is everything.
What you have given me
is everything
in return.

Now we are one being,
both of us giving
and receiving,
bound together
flame and candle
as before.

## 2.

### Only the Lovemaking

The Lover is always beside you,
waiting.

The Lover is patient,
like a devoted friend,
or someone who gave you food
long ago.

But you must give the signal.
You must say,
"Now, I am ready.
Come to my chamber at midnight."

The Lover will come,
still invisible,
still without a name.
Only the lovemaking
will be real.

**3.**

### Like Lovers of Shiva

When I come near you,
I fall backwards
in my joy.

There are waves
flowing
around your bodiless body,
scent coming
from your unfleshed flesh.

If you held me
in your arms,
I think that I
would perish,
the way the lovers
of Shiva
went up in flame
at the first glance.

*(Actually, the god/lover here is Zeus, but I am sure that somewhere there must be a similar myth about Shiva.)*

## 4.

## Or Even Sunsets

You say, all these proclamations of joy
are beginning to sound alike.

Tell me, can you tell one kiss
from another?
One night of pleasure
from the one before?

Or even sunsets.
Don't they begin to look alike
after so much looking?
Or the stars on different nights?

**5.**

**Whatever You Do**

Whatever you do,
don't tell anyone
about this.
They make laws against
such alliances,
put people in prison cells,
lock them away
like shadows.

They do not wish
to hear our story,
our tale must not be told.
Except, of course,
to those ready to listen,
the ones also enfolded
in this precious cloak,
tapestry embroidered
of god's flesh.

## APOLOGY

Do not think
that because I say words
to another,
that I have forsaken you:

love like ours
does not begin
or end
never fades
or disappears:

it is ours forever,
bound in the net
of eternal longing
no matter whose face
it may wear.

## CHRISTIAN MYSTICS

On the cover of the book,
pictures of the "Christian mystics,"
each one bearded,
heads uplifted
in attitudes of prayer.

In the meantime,
Teresa swoons in her raptures,
is visited by her
fiery angel,
hears the voice of God
speaking within

and Hildegard moves
through her garden,
gliding silent, or
sings
her holy hymns.

## PARTICLES DANCING

*"We are all writing God's poem."*
*Anne Sexton*

We are all
writing God's poem,
inscribing it onto our bodies,
breathing it into our cells.

Night and day
we make love with the light.
Where it is taking us,
we dare not ask.

We know only
that this is the love
that makes us
remember our beginnings,
particles dancing
in the holy fire.

## THE CELLULAR LEVEL

*"I will revel in a world
no longer particular."*
Elizabeth Spires

But of course, I never did.
Live in that world where
things had their own
particular name,
colors, definition.

Maybe it was because
my eyes were not sharp enough.
Things simply did not
stand out as much,
distinguish themselves
one from another.

For trees there were
pine, elm, and cotton wood.
Everything else relegated
to the compost pile
of the generic.

And as for flowers.
After daisy, rose,
hyacinth, I didn't
even try.
Though their beautiful
faces thrilled
as I passed along.

Strangely I could
remember other things—
names of poets, forms,
cadence.
Plots and mythological beings.
General categories of
thought,
universal concepts.
Plato's cave, the hero's journey.
Hybris and the fall of Oedipus,
the Goddess in her glory.
The veil of Maya hiding the perceived
world.
The night and day of Brahma,
the universe eternally reborn.

Yes, that's it.
More and more I lost notice
of the individual,
reduced everything,
to the generality
and fundamental myth,
then to feeling,
yearning for something more,
angels arriving in sheathes of light,
finally the cellular level,
rapture.

# HYMN TO THE NAMELESS ONE

It is true, yes,
that still I cannot name you.
Nor can I describe
your face,
never having seen it.
What I know is
that you have come
again and again,
often as something called
bliss,
or as landscapes pregnant with joy,
as sound like music
drifting from a shell.

Now as the year swings down,
and the darkness encloses
even the smallest bird,
the largest animal,
and we too enter the hour
when everything is falling once more
into the twilight
of not knowing,
what we ask is that
you be with us,
not as a pillar of fire
nor a blaze across
the heavens,
but like water
at rest in a pitcher
which catches the morning light
and is filled
with its own radiance.

# THE LEY LINES OF THE SOUL

Everything swept away.

What fire did not
devour,
flood consumed.

Nothing left but this
purified field,
this immaculate transparency.

The place where I
wait
for God.

# PART THREE

# HOW TO SEE AN ANGEL

## EVEN IF YOU HAVE TRUDGED

It is never too late.
Even if you have trudged
through snow and ice
for a thousand miles
and still have not arrived.
Even if the map is lost
and the compass broken.
When the eagle who is
supposed to guide you
goes off on a tangent
of its own
and you know you are,
once again, deserted
do not fall into
the pit of despair.
It will return,
brighter than ever.
There will be feather tokens
falling down.

Nothing is irredeemable.
Nothing is lost forever.
Be guided by the stars.
Let the moonlight
direct your steps.

There will be a path
which will open
in the forest.
The treasure which is yours
is waiting.

## IN A STRANGE TONGUE

Say you went on a journey
to a place
that was not on the map,
saw many strange sights there,
temples made of jade,
elephants with tusks of gold,
made love every night
with a different stranger.

Say you woke up one day,
found gold dust
in your pocket,
a bracelet of jade
wrapped around you wrist,
all else gone.

Who would listen
to your story?
Who would believe
your traveler's fairy tale?
Now you are
the outcast other,
the changeling
come home,
the revenant tapping
at the window,
speaking in a strange tongue
which no one understands.

## AFTER

There is one thing certain.
Once you have stood
in the midst of that
searing flame,
been struck down
to earth
like a pilgrim
entered by light at last
and have lain there,
waiting,
not quite certain—

how can you ever know again
what it is
not to be blinded by the light,
never to have gone there
to the top of the snow hung peak
and felt that nameless something
descend onto your shoulders,
your breast,
even as you bent forward
in disbelief.

## ST. TERESA REFLECTS ON HER RAPTURES

Sometimes I think
it might have been easier,
not to have been touched
by that stroke of fire,
not to have been consumed,
like Moses' bush, by that
flame that does not burn,
nor to have been lifted
to those storied heavens
where the gods look down
and never speak.

What does it mean to die
before death comes?
To arrive when the journey
has barely just begun?

How would life have been,
infused with the ordinary,
days worn thin with repetition,
children crying in the night,
bread rising, the wine jug filled,
as if by doing again and again
one might progress toward
an unknown goal?

On the chapel wall,
God stretches out his hand to Adam,
and Adam comes alive,
ready to be born once more.

How did you greet
that angel who arrived?
How did you bear it,
that shock of light,
when god entered every cell?

## TWO RIDDLES

Too vast
for human to
think it.

Too small
for human to
see it.

It lives
in the saint's ecstasy,
the lion's paw,

invisible as scent,
ever arriving
where it has
always been.

. . . . . . . . . . . . . . . . . . . . . . . . . . . . . . . . . . . . . .

You cannot define it.
You cannot measure it.

You cannot hold it.
You cannot give it away.

You cannot summon it.
You cannot dismiss it.

Some call it Buddha,
but it has no name.

## THE DISSIDENT

I am neither
Muslim nor Jew.

The ropes of Buddhism
do not trammel
my feet.

I refused the exalted ones
who instructed me to
bow down and kiss
their toes.

As for the Zens,
who wants to sit
on a hard mat
and stare at a wall
waiting for lightning
to flash.

Even the Taoists
had a handbook
of rules.

I tried breathing
and twisting
and saying magic words
but none of these helped.

Finally I heard a voice within
calling my name
and I fled into the Self of the self.

## AFTER ALL

*"Every year she got more like herself*
*and less like other people."*
*Flannery O'Connor*

After all,
it could have been different.
She could have been
the woman
whose seams
were always straight,
who looked through eyes
with 20/20 vision
and saw exactly
what the others saw,
no more, no less,
who never had thoughtful wrinkles,
or asked questions
of the oh so assured
workshop leader.
at the front of the room.

She could have been
the Sunday school teacher
with the quiet voice
who followed the lesson plan
line by line,
or the ashram devotee
arranging the flowers
and convinced that Baba
was God.

She could have opened wide
and swallowed
whatever it was
they offered
that day as truth,
or knelt down before
an image
that promised salvation.

But she would have
none of that.
Even if she had children,
a mate,
her questioning
didn't stop there.
She kept on looking,
searching,
keeping a secret diary.

Then one day it happened.
After that she knew
that rumors
of the heavens shuddering open,
of Light arriving in vast profusion,
that all the myths and fables
of humans mating with the unknown
were, in fact, real after all,
and she was now lifted
into that unknown realm.

## **BUDDHISTS**

They like order.
Guidelines
to discipline the soul.
They like words
like suchness, emptiness,
dependent origination.
Sometimes they will sit
in silence
until you think they are
a stone Buddha,
waiting through eternity
for something
to happen.
They have many vows,
ways of speaking,
moving,
dressing
to make them happy.

I am the sort
who would
not fit in.
I would step into the zendo
on the wrong foot,
need to go to the bathroom
at an inopportune time,
forget to tie my robe.
My back would hurt.
My feet would get restless.
start to move about.
I might burst into song

right in the middle of things
just to break the monotony,
or else nod off
and snore from
time to time.

I hear they have a stick
for people like me.

## ENOUGH

I think it is enough,
at times,
to go without knowing
where the end is,
what the beginning—
so long ago.

Perhaps you have friends
who can whisper
such things
in your ear,
hear little bits of
messages
in the laughter of children

But mostly we just proceed ahead,
not remembering
how it all started,
where it is leading,
not sure
if we are the waiting animal
or the animal's passing
shadow
in the grass.

## STONES PILED ONE ABOVE THE OTHER ON THE SHORE

I don't know who did this,
but see,
how they are balanced
so perfectly, each climbing
on the shoulders
of the other,
following the line
toward heaven.

At first,
I thought it was
a symbol of the chakras,
each mounting in turn
as they ascended
toward the one
ultimate illumination.

And then I discovered no,
the count was not right,
there was one—
or was it two?—
left over,
extended beyond the bounds,
making their own way upward.

But then I thought of Buddha,
how that spirit form sits
above the crown,
yet another Buddha poised
over him, and yet another
in infinite progression,

until at last
all Buddhas disappear,
vanish into
the nothingness
which is.

## SEA CHANGE

I cannot say
how I got caught up
on this wave,
bounding and tossing,
always farther out to sea,
always being shaped
into a new image,
meanwhile
my other familiar self
watching not so much
out of fear
but in curiosity and a casual interest
from the shore,
thinking,
Yes, now I am becoming
something other,
something more sturdy,
more flexible,
go ahead,
pound and mold me,
make me whatever it is
I am supposed to be
now at this time, in this place,
neither of which is locatable
on time pieces or maps,
both together forming a matrix
constantly shifting,
as if it can't quite make up its mind
where it wants to go,
or else has a purpose
that no one else
can see.

## *SPANDA KARIKA*

And so here we are,
a small dot
on the rim
of an inconsequential
planet,
sometimes caught in despair,
sometimes trembling
in joy.

Who would take notice
when we arrive,
when we go,
what our involvements are.

Yet it emerges,
something inside,
this flower that constantly
opens.

Only the pulsation
is real.

*(The* Spanda Karika *is the name of an
early text [ninth century?] of Kashmiri Shaivism,
a belief/spiritual practice which began in ancient India.
The term refers to the divine impulse or trembling
which creates and sustains the universe.)*

## EVERYTHING MOVING

Who am I to say
how this world
is put together,
how the seams and ridges
fit,
why the waters heave
and flow.

Only the architect
knows the full extent,
the weights and measures
of
the secret connections
in her palm.

Me, I have my corner
where I dance
to make the hours move,
rhythm to keep the sky alive,
hold earth and moon in place,
everything turning,
expanding sphere of light.

# EVER ARRIVING

*"At the still point of the turning world . . .*
*there the dance is . . .*
*Except for the point, the still point,*
*there would be no dance,*
*and there is only the dance."*
*T. S. Eliot*

I think of it
as the Swirling Radiance,
movement that never ceases,
ever arriving
from the last moment
of eternity,
the plundered second
of all that will ever be.

And you, here,
are at the midpoint,
the demarcation
of what has always been
and what is perpetually approaching,
your seeing is that which sustains,
carries forth,
enables.

You are the perpetual
witness,
heaven's link to time.
If you listen, you can
almost hear it swish
as it goes by.

## ABOUT NOTHING

The trouble with utterances like these
is that they are about nothing.

That is to say,
they are mainly about God
and everyone knows
that god is nothing—
not that, not that—
just an emptiness
a space between heartbeats or
notes on a page,
a single blank space
in the makeup of things
that you can never really
see or clearly define.

Successful poets
write about something—
the bread that didn't rise
properly,
the lover's groan,
the child who
cried in the night.
My problem, clearly,
is that I never learned to cook,
never planted a garden,
never went out to name
the passing birds.

My words will continue
to praise
nothing,

the presence that haunts me,
a net thrown out
in a sea
void of fish,
only these small flashing salt crystals
clinging to the ropey knots.

## IF YOU ARE A MYSTIC

If you are a mystic,
then you are from
an ancient and honorable tribe.

Whether you danced
alone
in your garden,
or celebrated
the rising moon,
whether you wrote verses,
of just felt the pulse
of the infinite
in your chest,
you are who I am now,
your child,
your begetter,
we are all from the
same place,
we dance
the same steps,
listen to the same music.

## BEFORE WE CAME

It is true
that when we first started out
everything was fiery.
Great lava flows
pouring down mountains,
cliffs breaking asunder
like pieces of flying stone
hurled from an unseen hand.

Then things got a bit quieter—
level plains,
soft meadows,
now and then a flower
or a flowing stream.

Now we travel
mostly by starlight
as if in a dream.
Sometimes we are not certain
if we are still plodding forward,
determined pilgrims moving ahead,
or resting somewhere
beside a quiet fire,
nestled in leaves.

What we know is that
this course
is the one we have chosen,
the map we drafted
before we even knew
about the treasure,
the vow we took
long before we came.

# AS SILK TO COARSE FIBER

(For the Beloved Within)

After a time
the awakening process settles down.
It is no longer strong feelings you want,
but something much
more subtle, more delicate,
refined.

As silk to coarse fiber,
as aged wine to heavy ale.

Something like
gentle breezes
after a strong wind.

The branches no longer
thrash and toss wildly,
threatening to break entirely
or demolish the houses
huddled below.

Even the clouds are still,
everything waiting
for this next new birth.

This is merely a metaphor—
how it felt in the beginning,
how it is between us now.

*(This poem is intended to describe the Kundalini process, which often begins in a rather stormy process, with much surging energy and many "ups and downs." As the years pass, things do indeed settle down, with the bliss flows becoming ever softer, arriving in subtle pulsations such as you would not have been able to experience at the outset.)*

## WHAT THE ANGEL SAID

At first it was relief.
At no longer having
that encumbrance of flesh,
the heavy weight pulling me down
into a kind of half-being,
thing of lightless clay.

Before,
I could not move
without such effort,
could not lift myself above
the curving surface
to which I was fastened.

O, I tried, but it was useless.
I rose a few feet higher at best,
and always the inevitable slow progression
from place to place.

Sometimes I wept at my immobility.
or strained to leave
my cell of flesh . . .
useless gesture.

Now, finally, I am free,
flitting from place to place
like a bee among honey buds,
an eagle soaring out of sight.
To think about a destination
is to arrive there,
to desire a shape
is to find oneself
remolded.

A flowing pulsation of gold veined light,
I wander among the remnants,
barely making out
the world I left behind.
I am glad I abandoned
all that uneasy furor,
that chaos of misdirected aims.

Yet sometimes I watch
and wonder
which is the better portion,
they with
their learning school
of grief and ambitions
which they share
with one another,
me with my lonely excess of love
always and ever the same.

*(Some think that angels are born into human form
now and again to be reminded of what it is to be earthbound.
Some also think that angels envy humans, for only in the
human sphere can spiritual progress be achieved.)*

## IF YOU WANT

If you want to feel
the sweet light
flow over your body,
then give yourself to light.

If you want
to taste the secret honey,
you must allow your throat
to open.

Moth to candle,
straw to flame,
you are nothing but
materials for burning.

## THE LIVES OF THE SOUL

are enigmatic, ethereal, ineffable—
as hard to capture
as catching the leaping fountain of God
in a teacup,
the flight of the eagle
into the sun,
the thunder of hooves
on the prairie
when the ears are closed
with candle wax.

The Soul arrives
in its own good time,
lets you know it is there
with a kiss on the lips,
a hand against your
breast.

If you can feel this,
then you know
that the Soul has come at last,
bringing its own
true gifts,
its inexplicable mercy.

## THE AWAKENING

You never knew
where it came from.
Later some said
past life,
some voted for purity
in this
(though you knew better).

In any event,
it was your time.
All the conditions were ripe,
floating like feathers
on a stream
to a preselected destination.

No one was there
to lead you.
Not even a person to tell,
friend or loved one,
attentive listener.
So you kept everything
locked in,
secret treasure
hidden in the
dark recesses
of your personal closet,
like a forbidden novel,
a store of some
illegal substance or thing.

Meanwhile,
you kept your appointments
each morning

with the unknown suitor,
the one you called the Beloved,
who had no name,
formless other.

As the years passed
you came to know
one another well in a fierce union,
flame of terror and bliss,
and the silence deepened.

You never discovered
why it happened,
what it meant.

Even now
it continues
in its own inscrutable
way.

Moment to moment
of the indecipherable.

## KARMA

*"There is another world*
*and it is inside this one."*
*Paul Eluard*

Buddha said to be a light unto yourself,
and so I followed the pathless path,
carving my way as I went.

Some said they needed containers
but I did not wish to be confined . . .
who would want to
be shut up in a cage?

I hurled all dogma
out the window,
did not spend time
sitting on cushions
contemplating nothing.

Instead I took off my clothes
and danced naked in my
living room, field of bliss,
as Buddha looked down
from the wall, smiling.

Day after day,
seduced by Krishna's flute,
Mirabai's honeyed syllables
I fed on amrita,
felt the unnamable
in the blood.

What else could I do?

# WHAT TO THINK OF BEFORE DYING

It could be a list of things—
things done and undone,
wills and thank you letters,
the cruise to the Greek Isles.

Or a catalogue of
best moments—
say when you stood
on the high mountain
at Mesa Verde
and saw the whole world
spread out
in a great circle beneath you
and for a few minutes
you knew how an eagle
must feel,
looking down
from an inestimable height,
and you almost rose
then and there.

Or entering the cave
at Carlsbad when
you were twelve,
the enveloping mystery,
the all consuming blackness
when they turned
the lights off.
How could anything,
even darkness,
be so ultimate?

Or standing there,
waiting to enter the spiraling mounds
at Tara,
the sweet energies
floating up out of the ground
through your very legs
and into your body.
Tasting the sacred.

And then there was that other,
the moment of revelation,
the one too deep to write about.
And you wonder
if it will follow you
as you go,
be your guide,
like a lantern held
by an invisible hand,
your own particular small
pillar of light
showing direction
into the arriving
unfathomable
as you wait
in wonder.

# DANCING WITH THE GREAT LION

I keep circling you,
pacing, checking
my watch.

You keep eyeing me,
growling in your throat,
saying, hurry, it's time.

How long have we been
doing this dance?
How many lifetimes
have we moved like this
together?

You suggesting,
me nodding,
both of us
waiting
to see what will happen.

## THE ANGEL

And if we should
perceive that
angel,
its blazing wings,
its shimmering hair,
let us have courage
to look
at it fully,
to feel
its radiant energies
as these flow
into who we are,
making us
more than we have
ever been
or imagined.

For an angel
is hard to bear.
What it demands
of us
greater than
the accustomed round.
What it wants
is nothing less
than everything,
relinquishment
of all the old ways,
heart opening
to a new creation,
self refashioned
into a more luminous design

## **GOING BEYOND**

Once you arrive at the crossroads,
you must choose
from three paths.

One is the path of fire.
To enter it,
you must take off
all your clothes,
fasten your tongue
to the roof of your mouth,
shut your eyes,
no longer breathe.

The second is the way of water.
To go here,
you must relinquish your boundaries,
make of yourself a drop of rain,
a splash of ocean water,
a handful drawn from a well.

The last is the journey by night
along earth's ridges and descents.
This will take a long time.
It will be filled with terrors,
fuming dragons,
monsters threatening.
When you finally arrive,
you will be nothing
but air,
mist,
burning sunlight,
you will be other.

# AUTHOR'S NOTE

Dorothy Walters lives and writes in Colorado, where she has a close relationship with the mountains as well as various streams and canyons. She has previously published two books of spiritual poetry as well as her own spiritual autobiography. Her article on "Kundalini and the Mystic Path" was included recently in "Kundalini Rising," an anthology from SoundsTrue press. She underwent major Kundalini awakening in 1981, and since that time has devoted her life to the unfolding of this process within herself and assisting others on a similar path through writing and other means. As someone who made her extensive journey without the direction of any external leader or guru, church, or established order, she is a strong believer in the "guru within," the inner guide rather than the external authority figure or institution. She feels that universal Kundalini awakening is the means for planetary and personal evolution of consciousness, and that evidence of planetary initiation is becoming more and more prevalent.

She produces a blog at *www.kundalinisplendor.blogspot.com*
(Poems and Reflections on the Spiritual Journey)

She may be contacted at dorothywalters72@yahoo.com
She is happy to hear from others undergoing deep spiritual transformation. Her Kundalini awakening and subsequent process of unfolding are described in her memoir "Unmasking the Rose, A Record of a Kundalini Initiation."

Her volumes of spiritual poetry are:

>"Marrow of Flame, Poems of the Spiritual Journey" and
>"A Cloth of Fine Gold, Poems of the Inner Journey"

CPSIA information can be obtained at www.ICGtesting.com
Printed in the USA
BVOW08s1952120416

443955BV00001B/27/P